electric guitar

ACKNOWLEDGEMENTS

Many, many thanks to: All my family and friends. Bruce, Damien and everyone at the Brighton Institute of Modern Music. Colin Campbell ('Morello' bass and mixing assistance). Tim Davies (Photography and Frisbee distractions). Gavin Fitzpatrick (Modelling and Widdle FX). Dan Partington ('Clapton' bass). Gerald Walton (Voice of 'Marshall' and Widdle FX). Rachael Wood (Modelling, proof reading, Widdle FX....and coffee). Jarry Hughes and Kenny Keith. www.AREmusic.co.uk

Printed in the United Kingdom by
MPG Books Ltd, Bodmin

Published by SMT, an imprint of
Sanctuary Publishing Limited
Sanctuary House
45–53 Sinclair Road
London W14 0NS
United Kingdom

www.sanctuarypublishing.com

ISBN: 1-84492-016-X

XTREME

electric guitar

Andrew Ellis

smt

CONTENTS

INTRODUCTION

Welcome to *Xtreme Electric Guitar*, your introduction to the instrument that we've all pretended to play in front of the mirror once or twice! There's a great mix of lessons, artist stories and style examples to get you up and running, all backed up with a CD to jam along to. We'll have plenty of fun and sneak in some important theory stuff too.

MEET YOUR TUTOR

We're very lucky to have Marshall as a tutor throughout this book. We've caught him on a break between world tours and he's keen to get you jamming. He'll explain the workings of the electric guitar and teach you the essential skills to work on. So, let's hand you over to the lord of the strings himself...

TRACK 1

MARSHALL IS HERE TO GUIDE YOU...

'Hey dudes, I'm Marshall. Yeah! It's a dream come true – I get to talk about guitar! You lot should be well pleased too 'coz you're gonna get an insight into some of my Xtreme riffs. I'll break it down and show you the way to rock stardom.

There are many different ways to play guitar but it all comes down to some common skills that we all need to know and master. We'll go through some lessons that will help you get those nailed and put your fingers into shape.'

ADVISE YOU...

'Well, you know I can demonstrate plenty of tricks but there's a world of totally inspiring guitarists out there to learn from too. Finding a guitar idol can move your playing on at an incredible pace. Just give me plenty of room on your poster wall, yeah?

We'll find out who the main strummers are and how they made their names in the music industry. We'll also look at how they do what they do and have a bit of a jam in their styles. Be sure to check 'em out – you are what you eat!'

TEST YOU...

'Oh man, not exams! OK, I hear you but it won't be like writing a history essay. This is where we'll check your progress and see just how close you're getting to my guitar-god status. I best get back to my practising too!'

MAKE YOU LAUGH...

'I don't know what I'd do without this bit of wood and strings. It's always by my side, although I have now learned to leave it outside the shower!

Hey this is gonna be sweeeet!'

YOUR ELECTRIC GUITAR

Ahhhh... isn't it a beauty?! But do remember that your guitar is not just about the paint job and funky shape.

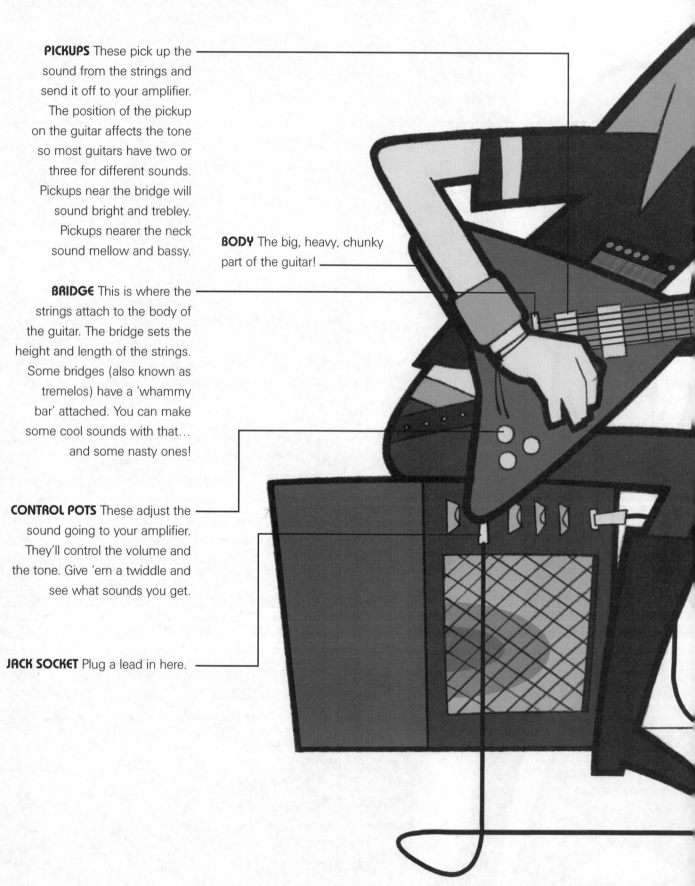

PICKUPS These pick up the sound from the strings and send it off to your amplifier. The position of the pickup on the guitar affects the tone so most guitars have two or three for different sounds. Pickups near the bridge will sound bright and trebley. Pickups nearer the neck sound mellow and bassy.

BRIDGE This is where the strings attach to the body of the guitar. The bridge sets the height and length of the strings. Some bridges (also known as tremelos) have a 'whammy bar' attached. You can make some cool sounds with that… and some nasty ones!

CONTROL POTS These adjust the sound going to your amplifier. They'll control the volume and the tone. Give 'em a twiddle and see what sounds you get.

JACK SOCKET Plug a lead in here.

BODY The big, heavy, chunky part of the guitar!

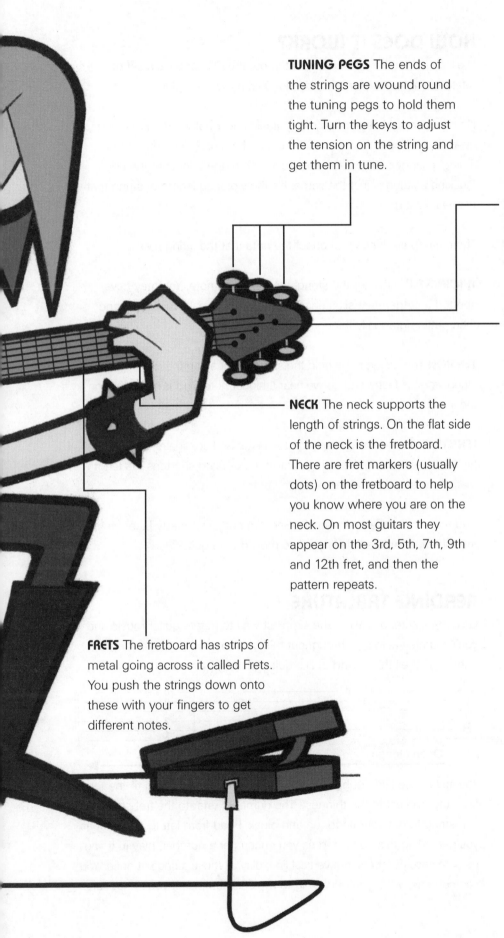

TUNING PEGS The ends of the strings are wound round the tuning pegs to hold them tight. Turn the keys to adjust the tension on the string and get them in tune.

HEADSTOCK The strings finish up here at the end of the neck. If you've got one with a pointy end, watch out for your band mates!

NUT This is kind of like a mini bridge at the end of the neck. It's where the strings vibrate to when you've got no fingers pressing down.

NECK The neck supports the length of strings. On the flat side of the neck is the fretboard. There are fret markers (usually dots) on the fretboard to help you know where you are on the neck. On most guitars they appear on the 3rd, 5th, 7th, 9th and 12th fret, and then the pattern repeats.

FRETS The fretboard has strips of metal going across it called Frets. You push the strings down onto these with your fingers to get different notes.

GET READY TO ROCK

HOW DOES IT WORK?

We'll check out how to tune up later, but the CD contains a set of reference notes so you can play along with my examples.

It's handy to understand why us guitarists do what we do. Have you ever tried 'boinging' a ruler on the edge of a table? The note of the 'boing' changes as you shorten the length of the ruler over the edge. Plucking a string is just the same. It's the vibrating length of string that we hear as a note.

There are three things that affect the note that the string makes:

THICKNESS The thicker the string, the lower the note. You may have spotted that there are six strings, starting with a really thick one, and then getting gradually thinner.

TENSION The tuning pegs hold the strings tight along the guitar. A tighter string vibrates faster and so we hear a higher note. This is how we tune the strings.

LENGTH A shorter string also vibrates faster and so, again, we hear a higher note. Pushing the strings onto the fretboard shortens the length that vibrates and therefore raises the note.

And that is how we make music. See, I'm not just a pretty face! I found the ruler and table a little limited so moved onto guitar.

READING TABLATURE

Guitar tablature, or TAB, is the simplest way to notate guitar music and you'll stumble across it throughout this book. You've done painting by numbers? Well this is kind of like guitar playing by numbers.

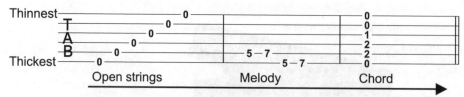

The strings are laid out horizontally, starting from the bottom to the top, from the thickest to the thinnest. The numbers refer to the fret space and string to put your finger on and pluck. Read from left to right just as you're reading this book, and as you encounter a number, play it! If you come across numbers in a vertical line, play all those strings at once. You can compare what you're playing to my CD examples if you're not sure.

HANDS

Just to make sure that both the right- and left-handed folk out there understand what I'm talking about:

FRET HAND The one holding the neck, pushing the strings onto the frets.
PICK HAND The one over the body, hitting the strings with the pick.

Some of the lessons require you to use specific fingers of your fret hand. Here's a hand diagram showing the numbers that we use – your index finger is number '1' and so on.

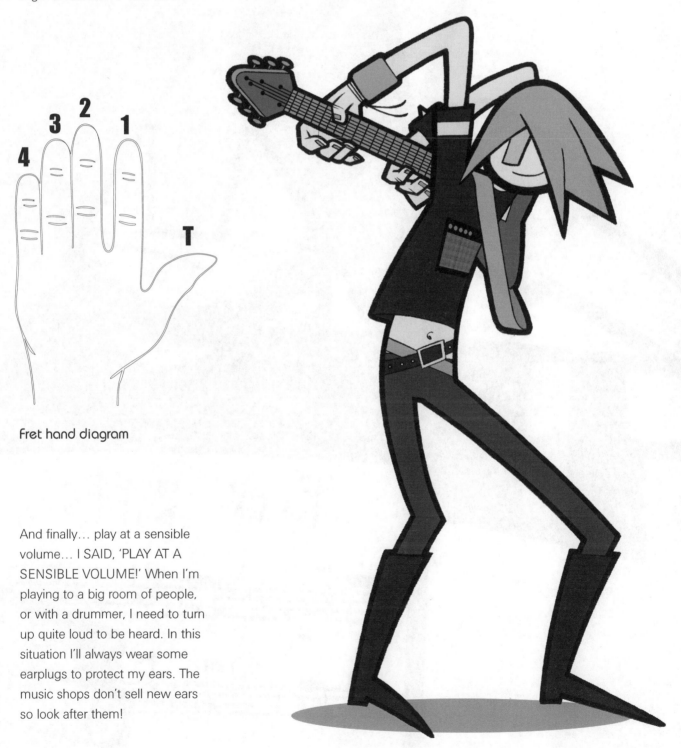

Fret hand diagram

And finally… play at a sensible volume… I SAID, 'PLAY AT A SENSIBLE VOLUME!' When I'm playing to a big room of people, or with a drummer, I need to turn up quite loud to be heard. In this situation I'll always wear some earplugs to protect my ears. The music shops don't sell new ears so look after them!

LESSONS

GET COMFORTABLE

Cool, you made it! This first lesson is all about making friends with your six-string and getting into some good habits straight away – it'll stand you in good stead for later when you're leaping about on stage. Now, your first steps on the guitar are likely to feel weird and quite a challenge, but learning to tie your shoelace was just the same, right?! Let's rock!

YOUR GOALS

GOAL 1
To hold the guitar correctly when sitting down and standing up.

GOAL 2
To get your hands in the correct positions.

GOAL 3
To make some noise!

THEORY

Take a close look at the photos for the position of the guitar, arms, hands, fingers and thumbs. All these bits need to come together to make a good playing style.

Correct playing position when seated

Correct playing position when standing

IN PRACTICE

Right, let's see how you look. At the beginning, don't dance around too much – an electric guitar is a bit heavier than an air guitar!

STEP 1

Always try to keep your back straight. If you're sitting down, rest the guitar body on your right leg (left-handers on your left leg). When standing up, your strap height is all about the balance between looking cool and playing without getting a strain. The height in the picture (see p15) is ideal as the guitar position matches closely to that when seated. If you make sure you don't feel too tense when playing, you'll have got it about right.

STEP 2

The main purpose of the fret hand is to push the strings down against the metal frets, with the fingertip just above them. Get your fingers and thumb roughly parallel to the frets and squeeze with your thumb behind the neck. Imagine you've got your hand in a glove puppet that's trying to take a bite out of the neck!

STEP 3

Your fret elbow shouldn't be tucked into your body, nor should it be stuck out like a chicken wing – try somewhere in-between. Check the photos (see p15).

STEP 4

The pick hand is for getting the strings to vibrate. Hold the pick between the first finger and thumb and hit the strings with the pointy end. Big strums should come from twisting your wrist and bending your elbow. Smaller, single-string picks come from your fingers, thumb and again the twisting wrist.

We'll look at all this in more detail in the following lessons.

PROBLEM?

If it hurts, stop. Stretch out or take a rest. These are new movements to your fingers, wrists and arms. Your fingertips will get sore but after a few weeks they'll build up a tougher layer of skin to deal with the new activity.

EXERCISE

OK, I'm gonna let you loose. Some of the best riffs come from messing around, so give it a go. I've done the same on the CD track to help you feel at home. Experiment!

1. Strum across all the strings. Don't worry too much about getting nice sounds for the moment – maybe do this at low volume to avoid complaints!

2. Pick individual strings. Try to keep a part of your picking hand in contact with the guitar body so you don't miss your target.

3. Hit the strings hard or pluck them softly. Get some percussive sounds and stop notes ringing by resting your fret hand lightly over the strings.

4. Make use of all four fingers on the fretboard. You'll probably have one finger that's particularly badly behaved. Keep trying – it'll get the message sooner or later.

TIP

Practise standing up as well as sitting down. Get a music stand so your books are at eye level. This will stop you playing like the Hunchback of Notre Dame – he was only famous for ringing bells.

TEST

QUESTION 1
What should you do if things start to hurt?

QUESTION 2
Which leg should you rest the guitar on when seated?

QUESTION 3
What is a good technique to ensure accurate picking?

QUESTION 4
Which hand is your picking hand?

TUNE UP

Dudes, it doesn't matter if you're playing country or heavy metal – you need to get your guitar in tune. If you don't, it's gonna stink!

YOUR GOALS

GOAL 1
To remember the note each string is tuned to.

GOAL 2
To train your ears to recognise the difference between two notes.

GOAL 3
To get the guitar in tune.

GOAL 4
To understand how to use an electronic tuner.

THEORY

First things first – you need to memorise the note each string is tuned to. The standard tuning is shown below.

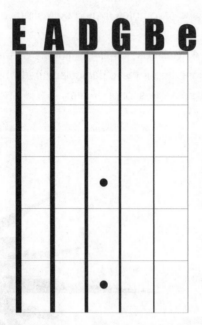

To help yourself remember, use a phrase such as:

EVERY ANGRY DOG GROWLS BEFORE EATING

Make up your own phrase if you don't like dogs!

So now I should be able to say, 'Play the D string' and you'll know what to do. Also, I hope you've noticed we've got two E strings. We call the thicker string with the lower pitch 'low E' and the thin string with the higher pitch (two octaves higher) 'high E'. Sorted.

Tuning up is going to involve training your ears to recognise if two notes sound the same. When their pitches are far apart it should be reasonably obvious. When they are the same they should almost sound like one. If the notes are very close to each other you might hear a pulsing sound as they interfere with each other – these pulses are known as 'beats'. Listen for this effect to tell you that the strings are nearly in tune. If a note is tuned too high we say that it is 'sharp' and if it's too low we say that it is 'flat'.

IN PRACTICE

We're going to learn to tune up with a technique called 'relative tuning'. One string is tuned by listening to a reference note, perhaps from a piano. With that string correct, you tune the other strings from it. Check it out:

STEP 1

Listen to the tuning track on the CD (Track 2) to hear what the low E string should sound like (or play another instrument's E). Play your low E string and adjust its tuning peg until they sound the same. This is now your reference note on the guitar. When you're in a band, make sure you all tune to the same reference note otherwise the audience will be running for the exit.

STEP 2

So how do we know what the A string should sound like? Well, if you play the fifth fret of the E string that we just tuned, it will give us A. Therefore, play that to hear the note we're aiming for and then play the A string to hear the difference. Adjust the A string's tuning peg until it sounds the same.

PROBLEM?

Does your guitar have a tremolo (a bridge with springs in the back that moves up and down)? If so, when you've tuned all six strings, the tension on the springs will have changed and moved the bridge slightly. You might need to go through the six steps a few times to get it bang-on in tune.

STEP 3

Now that the A string is in tune we can use it to tune the D string.
This time play the fifth fret of the A string and it will give us a D.
You guessed it – tune the D string to this.

STEP 4

Next, the G string can be tuned to the fifth fret of the D string.

STEP 5

Now that you're getting used to this pattern, it's time to be
awkward. With the G string now in tune, we use it as our
reference to tune the B string, but this note is on the fourth fret of
the G string (not the fifth like we have been doing).

STEP 6

For the final high E string, we go back to the old formula of playing
the fifth fret of the B string to give us the note E. Job done.

To check that all went well, it's best to give your favourite chord a
strum and see if it sounds sweet (we'll come to chords later). If it
makes you pull a face, repeat the steps to fine-tune everything.

EXERCISE

1. Below is the fifth-fret tuning method written out in tablature. This is demonstrated on the CD.

Listen out for the open strings that initially sound out of tune and then get adjusted to match the reference note.

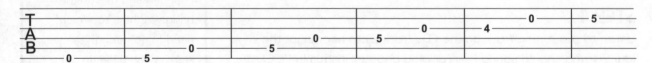

2. You can also use the tuning track on the CD to tune up all the strings as I play through them.

TIP

When you need to tune quickly and quietly it's best to use an electronic tuner. Plug your lead in, make sure the guitar's volume is up and pluck a string. A needle or light indicates the note and whether it's sharp, flat or in tune. Try not to neglect the fifth-fret method though as you don't want to be dependent on a little box of tricks.

Below are a couple of examples of electronic tuners:

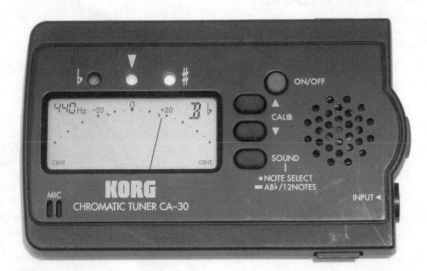

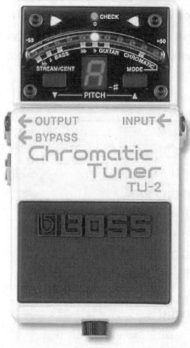

TEST

QUESTION 1
What phrase can you use to remember the string tunings?

QUESTION 2
Which string do we tune with the fourth fret of the previous string?

QUESTION 3
Which fret do all the other strings tune from?

EAR TRAINING I'll play ten pairs of notes on the CD. See if you can work out if the second note of each pair is sharp, flat or in tune. If you've got a music buddy, test each other with your own choice of notes.

TRACK 7

PICKING

When the strings vibrate, the guitar sounds great... OK, I get ya – more guitar, less rap! Electric guitar is usually played with a triangular piece of plastic called a 'pick' or 'plectum'. Some people have been known to play with coins but they're very solid and not very pointy. If you hand a coin over to the kind person in your local music shop, they'll exchange it for a proper pick – what a deal! They come in many different colours, but more importantly various thicknesses. See how you get on with a medium thickness – anything too thin and it's like trying to play with a piece of paper.

YOUR GOALS

GOAL 1
To hold the pick correctly.

GOAL 2
To support your pick hand.

GOAL 3
To pick individual strings accurately and in time.

GOAL 4
To try out different picking directions.

THEORY

Take a look at these photos to see how to grip a pick.

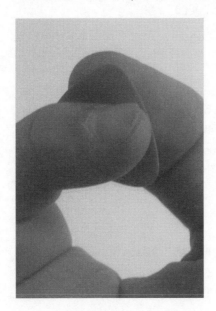
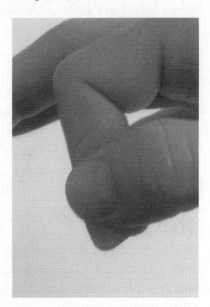

PICKING TECHNIQUE

The pointiest part of the pick should come out from the side of your thumb. Grip the pick against the thumb with the side of your first finger curled behind.

We're looking at picking individual strings in this lesson so you need to be accurate. Each string is quite a small target so try to keep your hand as close to the guitar body as possible. To help, you can anchor your little finger down on the guitar body or rest the heel of your hand on the bridge – make sure it doesn't mute the string you want to play though.

IN PRACTICE

Give it a go then. Grab the pick and be sure not to drop it – they have a nasty habit of vanishing into carpets!

STEP 1

Choose a string, hold your pick above it and then push through in a downward motion towards the floor. The movement should come from a combination of bending your thumb and first finger along with a bit of wrist. We're aiming for just the one string so try to stop before you hit another one below it. These are called 'downstrokes'.

STEP 2

Now try to pick the string at regular intervals – eg every second a clock ticks. Choose a slow pace that you're comfortable with to start with and only speed up when you're in control and accurate – it'll take a while to get used to the feel.

STEP 3

When you're happy with the downstrokes, try the opposite… an 'upstroke'! Start the pick below the chosen string and move up through it. Again, try this to a regular beat and aim for accuracy rather than speed.

STEP 4

Experiment with different volumes by hitting the strings hard and then plucking them softly.

STEP 5

Finally, if you're confident with the down and upstrokes separately, try combining the two motions, one after the other – downstroke then upstroke, down, up, down, up, down, up. This is known as 'alternate' picking and will improve the speed of your picking as it's very efficient.

PROBLEM?

You might find the pick snagging on a string, causing you to lose time or hit other strings when it finally pops out. Firstly, most of the pick is there for you to hold rather than hit the string with – just pick the string with the tip. You can control this by only showing a small amount of the pick from the side of your thumb. Secondly, experiment with the pick angle so that it can almost slide off the string.

TIP

When recording in the studio, they often make you play along to a click. This will help the band sound tight and the engineers will be able to do all their computer whiz stuff. Work on your timing by playing along with something that gives you a regular beat – a metronome, drum machine or piece of music with an even tempo.

EXERCISE

1. This exercise should give you a feel for where each string is. Start on the low E and move from one string to the next. Upon reaching the high E, reverse the pattern and head back.

At the start and end of this example you'll spot double bar lines with two dots. These are repeat marks and basically mean when you get to the end, start again.

TRACK 8 CD

2. This pattern is very similar to the previous one but we're going to pluck the same string four times before moving onto the next.

Try playing the first note of each group a bit louder than the other three. Count along with each pick – '1, 2, 3, 4, 1, 2, 3, 4, etc' (shouting the 1s).

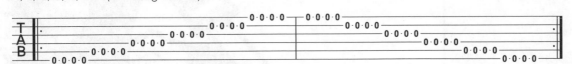

TRACK 9 CD

3. Here is an exercise that involves a bit of string skipping. Try to make sure that you don't hit the string in-between. You can remember the first half of the pattern by thinking 'skip one, back one, skip one, back one', and then reverse it for the trip back.

TRACK 10 CD

For each of these exercises try the different picking techniques we've learned – downstrokes, upstrokes and alternate.

TEST

QUESTION 1
What part of the pick should be hitting the string?

QUESTION 2
How can you make sure you hit the right string without looking?

QUESTION 3
What can you use to practise playing in time?

QUESTION 4
What is the benefit of alternate picking?

FRETTING

Well, you might be getting a bit bored with only a choice of six notes. Now that your pick hand is starting to get familiar with the strings, we can turn our attention to the fret hand. Let's go for a jog on the fretboard!

YOUR GOALS

GOAL 1
To position your fret hand and fingers correctly.

GOAL 2
To make your fingers strong and flexible.

GOAL 3
To get the notes ringing out clearly.

GOAL 4
To learn some finger patterns.

THEORY

To fret a note, your fingertip should push the string down towards the fretboard so that it makes contact with the metal fret. Keep your thumb behind the neck so you've got something to press against.

FRETTING TECHNIQUE

The ideal position for your finger is just before the fret wire. If the finger is too far away, the note will buzz. If the finger is too close it will stop the string vibrating below the fret and you won't hear very much at all.

FRETTING TECHNIQUE IN PRACTICE

This is a bit like going to the finger gym. It's no different to making your legs take you out for a run, so start slowly and gradually build up.

STEP 1

The first thing that all musical athletes should do is to make sure that they're warm. Wiggle the fingers, and stretch out the arms and wrists.

STEP 2

Now let's try for a note. Put your first finger down on the fifth fret of the A string. Give the string a pick and see what you get. If you're not pushing the string down hard enough it'll buzz and you'll feel it rattle under your finger. However, don't push too hard because that will hurt and the string will bend causing the pitch to change and all your efforts in the tuning lesson will be wasted!

STEP 3

Now try the sixth fret with your second finger, then the seventh fret with your third finger. Don't forget your little finger gets a turn on the eighth fret.

STEP 4

Do you see that your fingers have lined up over the fifth, sixth, seventh and eighth frets? This is called the 'finger-per-fret' technique. By doing this you should find that you don't have to move your hand up and down the neck and can play any of those four frets without having to look.

TIP

Take a close look at the fretboard and you should see that as the frets go up the neck (towards the guitar body), they get closer together. If you're finding these exercises a bit of a stretch, try the patterns higher up. As your fingers get more flexible they'll be able to reach further, eventually being able to play the patterns right down at the first fret – ooooof!

STEP 5

Try this technique on different strings and different frets.

TEST

QUESTION 1
Where should your finger fret the string?

QUESTION 2
Which is your weakest finger? See if you can come up with an exercise that helps it catch the others up.

QUESTION 3
Why do we want to work on the finger-per-fret technique?

Make up your own exercise patterns to help you become a fret wizard.

EXERCISE

1. Now we're going to move on a small step from the four-picks-per-string in the last lesson. This time have your first finger fret the string you're picking at the fifth fret. On the way back down, move up to the sixth fret.

Start slowly and make sure each note rings out clearly without any buzzing or rattling. Try the exercise with each finger and get used to the feeling. Experiment on different frets too.

```
                              5-5-5-5 - 6-6-6-6
                     5-5-5-5          6-6-6-6
T            5-5-5-5                      6-6-6-6
A       5-5-5-5                              6-6-6-6
B   5-5-5-5                                      6-6-6-6
```

2. The aim of this exercise is to work on the finger-per-fret system. It starts with your first finger on the fifth fret, second finger on the sixth, third finger on the seventh and fourth finger on the eighth. These fingerings are shown above the TAB.

When you get to the high E string, shift all your fingers up one fret by moving your hand along the neck. Your little finger should be on the ninth fret and ready to reverse the pattern to come back down.

```
    1  2  3  4   1  2  3  4 ........
                              5-6-7-8 - 9-8-7-6
                     5-6-7-8          9-8-7-6
T            5-6-7-8                      9-8-7-6
A       5-6-7-8                              9-8-7-6
B   5-6-7-8                                      9-8-7-6
```

3. A small variation on the last exercise is to play just three notes per string. Again, try to keep with the finger-per-fret system – keep all your fingers involved. There should be as little hand movement as possible.

Don't forget that these exercises are still working on your picking skills. Give this one a try with the alternate picking – an odd number of picks per string can take a bit of getting used to.

```
                           5-6-7 - 8-7-6
                    5-6-7          8-7-6
T           5-6-7                      8-7-6
A      5-6-7                               8-7-6
B   5-6-7                                      8-7-6
```

4. Sticking with the finger-per-fret idea, this example requires you to move all your fingers along a fret as you change string. Just watch out for the slight change in pattern between the G and B strings – they stay on the same frets.

You should be able to hear the note is going up in small steps each time until you reach the top. This is known as a 'chromatic' scale because it includes every single note between the start and the finish.

```
                            3-4-5-6 - 7-6-5-4
                    4-5-6-7          8-7-6-5
T           4-5-6-7                      8-7-6-5
A       5-6-7-8                              9-8-7-6
B     6-7-8-9                                10-9-8-7
    7-8-9 10                                   11-10-9-8
```

Use these exercise patterns to strengthen fingers and improve co-ordination. The patterns are relatively simple to remember so you can concentrate on the physical side. Don't forget to try playing in time to a metronome or drum beat.

OPEN CHORDS

So far it's all been about tuneless single notes, but you've had enough to think about trying to get those fingers to behave, yeah? They should be starting to get the message now so we'll move on a bit. The guitar has one, two, three, four, five… six strings so let's see what happens when we play them all at once. No, not just all the open strings! We'll need to learn some chord shapes first so it sounds good.

YOUR GOALS

GOAL 1
To learn to read chord charts and diagrams.

GOAL 2
To memorise some open chord shapes.

GOAL 3
To get familiar with the chord sounds.

GOAL 4
To get all the strings ringing clearly – flex those fingers!

THEORY

We're going to learn some 'open' chords. By this we mean that some of the strings are fretted with the fingers but some are left to ring untouched. A chord is a group of notes played together, and if you pick the right notes it sounds great. The chord shapes in this lesson give us some of the good combinations of notes to play.

To show chords we use chord diagrams that have the six strings from left to right – 'E, A, D, G, B, E' (remember the phrase?). The thick line going across the top is the nut at the end of the neck and then we have the first, second and third fret (indicated with the fret marker).

Basically, put your finger where you see a circle! The number in the circles is the best finger to use so you don't get into a tangle. Play all the strings with your pick hand unless there's an 'X' above it.

Chords can be powerful things. If you play the right ones, you can make people smile or cry! Major chords tend to give a happy sound. Minor chords have a sad sound. Listen out for this.

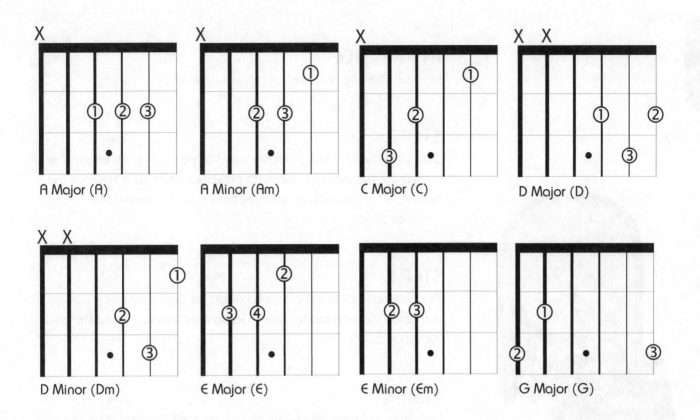

A Major (A)   A Minor (Am)   C Major (C)   D Major (D)

D Minor (Dm)   E Major (E)   E Minor (Em)   G Major (G)

LEFT-HANDERS

Chord charts are always drawn for righties. You'll need to get used to reflecting them in your head so the strings and shapes are the other way round as on your left-handed guitar. The string thicknesses are drawn on these charts to help you find your way. Try angling a small mirror alongside them to get the idea.

PROBLEM?

If a chord isn't sounding great, pick each string individually and check it's ringing clearly. Don't give up! Getting all the notes to ring properly is quite difficult to start with but you'll gradually get a feel for it. Here's a checklist:

1. Are all your fingers on the correct strings and frets as in the chord diagram? Make sure that you haven't got two fingers on the same string – that don't do much!

2. Is another finger muting a string by resting against it?

3. Are all your fingers positioned in the fret spaces properly? Check back to the fretting lesson.

4. Make sure you're putting the correct amount of pressure on each of the strings.

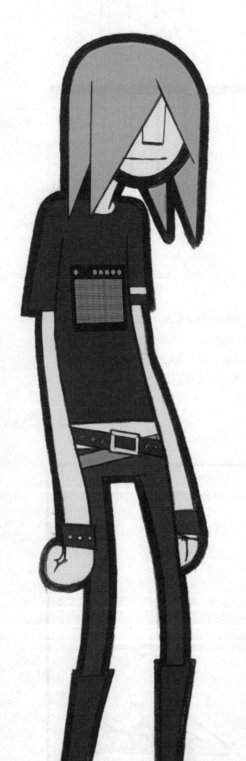

IN PRACTICE

Here are some helpful hints that should make things easier.

STEP 1

Choose a chord! You'll probably need to position each finger one by one for the moment, but with practice they'll start to learn the positions for themselves and you'll be able to plonk them all down at once.

STEP 2

Try to bring your fingers in at an angle so they only make contact with the intended string. Aim to keep your thumb behind the neck for support.

STEP 3

Let's have a listen. Hold your pick at the first thick string in the chord and strum down through all of them in one movement.

STEP 4

Take all your fingers off and then go back to the chord shape again. As you learn more chords, practise going from one to another.

STEP 5

To help memorise the chords, look for patterns in them. For example, join the dots to see that D major makes a triangle and notice that there's just a small difference between E major and E minor.

TIP

You don't have to strum all the strings in a chord at once. If you're only strumming a couple there's nothing to say your fingers have to fret the entire shape either. Try playing just small parts of these chord shapes and see what you get – eg the D, G and B strings.

EXERCISE

1. Try to spot which chords these are from their TAB representation, then have a listen to the CD. Remember that if the numbers are all in a line, you play them all at the same time.

This example has each chord played firstly as an 'arpeggio' and then strummed. An arpeggio is when the individual strings are plucked one by one.

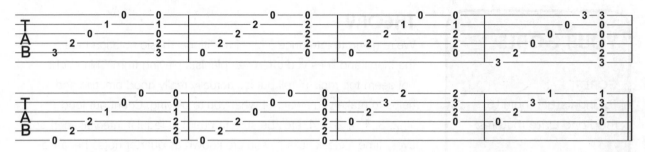

2. Here's a chord chart. There's a chord written in each bar. If you see a chord note written by itself, it's major. A small 'm' after it means it's minor.

For each bar, count '1, 2, 3, 4' and strum on each count. Count at a slow pace to start with and try to keep it regular. Try to look ahead and prepare in your head for the next chord that's coming up.

| G | Em | C | D | G | Dm | Am | E |

Have a go at making up some of your own chord progressions.

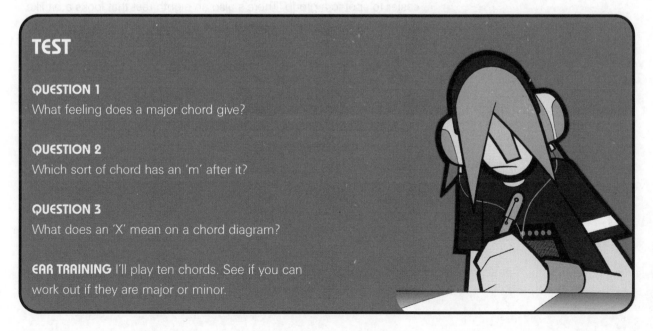

TEST

QUESTION 1
What feeling does a major chord give?

QUESTION 2
Which sort of chord has an 'm' after it?

QUESTION 3
What does an 'X' mean on a chord diagram?

EAR TRAINING I'll play ten chords. See if you can work out if they are major or minor.

STRUMMING

Now that you're armed with some big chords, let's look at some methods of strumming them and work on rhythm patterns to get a bit of a groove on...

YOUR GOALS

GOAL 1
To understand how to read and write rhythms.

GOAL 2
To learn some strumming patterns.

GOAL 3
To play in time.

GOAL 4
To control the strings with muting.

THEORY

We're going to introduce a bit of traditional music notation here – the blobs and lines you often see pianists playing from. This might not seem too rock 'n' roll but it's actually really good practise and helps to make you aware of what you're playing. Count out loud '1, 2, 3, 4, 1, 2, 3, 4, etc'. Be sure to count at regular intervals, perhaps every time a clock ticks. These are known as quarter notes because there are four of them to each bar. Tap your foot with each count so that you're feeling the beat and then start the count again. The symbol for a quarter note is the stick with a blob on the end, also known as a 'crotchet'. If you see the squiggly symbol, it still represents a count of '1' but is a 'rest', so you don't play a note.

♩ crotchet   𝄽 rest

Now keep the same count at the same speed but in-between each number say 'and'. So you'll be counting '1 and 2 and 3 and 4 and'. Keep your foot tapping on the numbers and feel the 'and' going in the space. These are eighth notes because there are now eight of them in a bar. An eighth note, also known as a 'quaver', looks similar to the crotchet symbol but it has a little tail hanging off. If there are two of them next to each other, the tails are linked together so that they're easier to spot in a group. There's also an eighth rest that looks a bit like the number 7, so count it but don't play.

♪ quaver   ♫ two quavers   ♧ rest

It can be good practice to give the count of '1' a bit of extra oooomph to indicate the start of each bar.

IN PRACTICE

So now that we can count quarter and eighth notes, it's time to get the guitar involved.

STEP 1

Mute all the strings with your fretting hand by resting the fingers lightly over the fretboard. Don't push the strings down because they'll still make a note. Strum the pick down all the strings. This is a downstroke, just like when we were picking single strings. It is notated with a ⊓ symbol. Try an upstroke. This is notated with a ∨ symbol. With the muting you should just be getting a percussive sound with no ringing strings.

STEP 2

Go back to counting quarter notes – '1, 2, 3, 4'. For each count, strum a downstroke. When you bring your arm up for the next downstroke, make sure that you don't hit the strings. Get a feel for that and keep your foot tapping. Nod your head, too, if you like.

STEP 3

Now we'll go to eighth notes – '1 and 2 and 3 and 4 and'. Keep strumming the downstrokes as you were before but hit the strings on your way back up. These upstrokes become the 'ands' in-between the numbers.

STEP 4

Now leave out the downstrokes so that you're only strumming up on the 'ands'. On the numbers, keep your foot tapping and arm going down (but missing the strings). This is called playing on the 'offbeat'.

STEP 5

We've done all this with your fret hand muting the strings to help concentrate on the strumming. Now try these steps with some of the open chords learned earlier.

PROBLEM?

Trouble keeping time? Your strums will stay on the beat if you keep your arm ticking up and down, even when not hitting the strings. Keep a nice smooth strumming motion at all times – no stopping and starting. You don't need the accuracy of single-string picking here so try using more elbow for the motion. A big heavy grunge style would even use the shoulder to get more energy into the strings.

EXERCISE

I'm going to play all these exercises for you with the G major open chord. Get used to the rhythms and then experiment with some of the other chords and progressions we've looked at.

Each example has the traditional notation at the top. Below that is the down or upstroke symbol. Underneath those is how to count along.

1. Quarter notes – downstrokes regularly on the beat.

2. Eighth notes – downstrokes in the same places as before but with upstrokes in-between to make it twice as fast.

3. Offbeat – eighth notes but only the upstrokes are strummed. Miss the strings on the downstrokes.

4. Now we start to mix them up for more interesting rhythms.

5. Complicated rhythms now. Keep your arm ticking and watch the count.

TIP

We started this lesson by muting the strings with our fretting hand. You can use this technique to control the length of notes. If you want a chord to only ring out for a moment, strum it and then rest either hand lightly over the strings to stop them vibrating. Muting can be used to create some interesting rhythms and to bring a bit more control to your playing. After a while, muting becomes instinct and you won't even realise that you're doing it. Doing what?... eh?

6. Complicated rhythms now. Keep your arm ticking and watch the count.

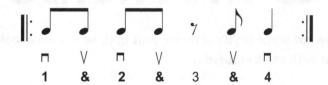

QUESTION 1
What note value is a crotchet?

QUESTION 2
Which symbol indicates an upstroke?

QUESTION 3
How can you stop the strings ringing?

Write out all the eighth notes '1 and 2 and 3 and 4 and'. Scribble out a few beats of your choice, making them rests. See if you can play the new rhythm that you've made.

KNOW THE FRETBOARD

Now that you've got some rhythms under your belt, let's have a look at what's going on with the fretboard…

YOUR GOALS

GOAL 1
To use the fret markers to find your way.

GOAL 2
To understand the musical alphabet.

GOAL 3
To learn the notes on the fretboard.

THEORY

The fret markers aren't there just to look pretty. These are the dots (or sometimes other symbols) that help us to quickly find the fret number that we want. Imagine if the fretboard was just plain – to find fret 11, you'd have to start at the bottom and count up one by one. The rest of the band would have finished the song by the time you'd got there!

Fretboards usually have single dots on the third, fifth, seventh and ninth fret followed by a double dot on the twelfth. The pattern then repeats until the guitar runs out of neck.

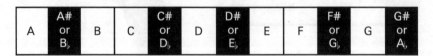

So now when I ask for fret 11, you can find the double dot (fret 12) and go one below it. Fair play dudes, that was much quicker! Try to find more shortcuts like that.

We've been encountering letters to describe notes and chords, so let's have a look at this in more detail. Musical notes are given letters of the alphabet. The good news is that they don't go all the way up to Z. They go from A to G and then start again. The weird bit is that there are notes in-between called 'sharps' or 'flats'. A sharp note has the '#' symbol after it, a flat note has a '♭' symbol. This tends to make more sense to pianists but us shredders need to have a grasp of it too:

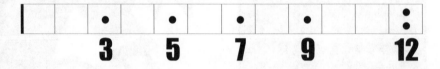

Notice that there isn't a sharp/flat note from 'B to C' and 'E to F'. Memorise that and you're well on your way.

IN PRACTICE

Let's have a look at the low E string and figure out where the other notes are.

STEP 1

Work your way up the E string, playing at each fret and saying the notes out loud to make sure you're thinking about it – don't be lazy now, it does help!

STEP 2

Remember when we were tuning up that we tuned the A string by listening to the fifth fret of the E string? Well there it is in black and white – the fifth fret of the E string is the note A. You knew that already, right?

STEP 3

Do you see that you get right back to the original note at the 12th fret? – this is known as the 'octave'. Play the open string and then the 12th fret. You should hear that they sound similar but one is pitched higher than the other.

STEP 4

Fill in the gaps. The spaces between labelled notes are the sharps or flats – eg between A and B you have A# (or B♭). The A is sharpened (raised in pitch a semitone) or the B is flattened (lowered in pitch by a semitone).

STEP 5

Good news! – Learning the low E string gives you two bits of knowledge for the price of one because there are two E strings! Therefore, the notes on the high E string are in the same places. Result!

Now try the same steps with the A string.

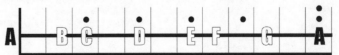

To help remember these it's all about looking for patterns and associating the fret markers with the fret numbers and the notes.

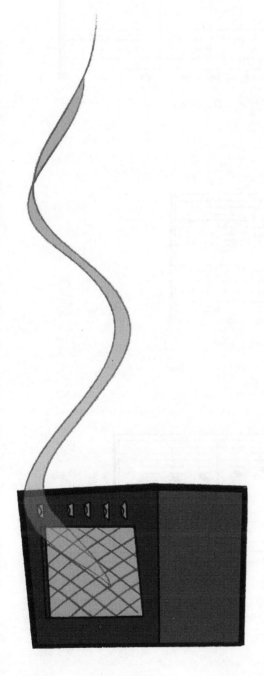

EXERCISE

These exercises also have traditional notation above the TAB so you can see where the notes appear on a stave and when a sharp or flat note occurs. Don't let it scare you though!

1. Work your way up the E string fret by fret and say the notes out loud. This is another chromatic scale like we saw back in the picking lesson.

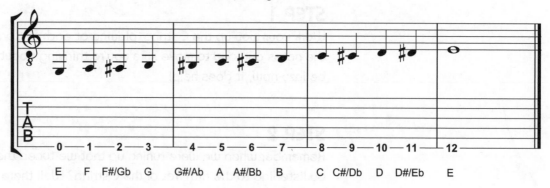

2. This example is playing on the fret markers.

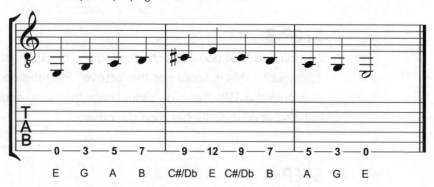

3. There are no sharps or flats in this section.

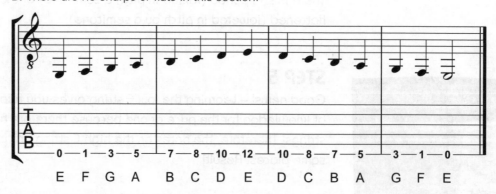

PROBLEM?

Yes, I know! Memorising one string is tricky enough. Here's a shortcut to get some more string notes from what you already know. Pick a note on the low E string and then play two frets higher on the D string. This is an octave and hence the same note name. So you can now find the same notes on the D string reasonably quickly. The same shape works for the A and G strings.

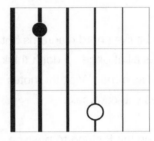

E to D string octave

A to G string octave

TIP

You know your 'ABC', yeah? Learn your 'CBA'! What I mean is, if you're playing down the neck it can be extra handy to be able to recite the musical alphabet backwards – 'G, F, E, D, C, B, A'. Whoa!

TEST

QUESTION 1

Which notes have no sharp/flat note between them?

Write out a list of random notes and then try to find them one by one.

QUESTION 2

Which note is an octave up from B?

Work out the notes on the strings that we haven't looked at.

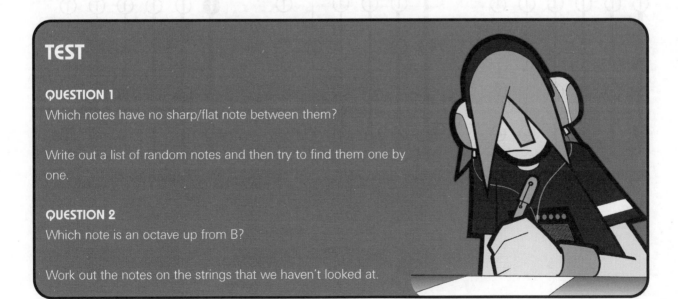

SCALES

In the previous lessons we've encountered the chromatic scale, which includes all 12 notes – not very imaginative. Within a song, some of these notes will sound good but some of them will sound bad. We use scales to show us where the right notes are for the sounds that we want.

THEORY

The scale diagrams in this lesson look a little bit like chord diagrams but you are not intended to play the marked notes all at once – I don't think you've got enough fingers! You can use them as a map. Visit the notes in whatever order you like and see what tunes you can make.

We use what we've learned about the notes on the E string to position the scale shapes. The black dots on the scale diagrams indicate the 'root' note – the first note in the scale. Unlike the open chords, you can move these shapes anywhere on the guitar neck. So, if you start with the black dot on the fifth fret of the E string, you're playing in the key of A. With the black dot on the eighth fret, you're playing in the key of C. The rest of the dots fall around this, as arranged on the diagrams.

The notes in a major (diatonic) and major pentatonic scale will fit nicely with a major chord backing it in the same key – eg G major pentatonic with a G major chord. The minor pentatonic works well with major or minor chords of the same key. Remember from the chords we learned that major has a happy sound and minor has a sad sound.

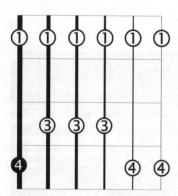

Major pentatonic

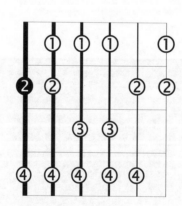

Major (diatonic)

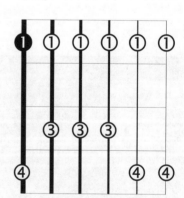

Minor pentatonic

YOUR GOALS

GOAL 1
To learn some scale shapes.

GOAL 2
To get used to their sounds.

GOAL 3
To improve picking and fretting.

GOAL 4
To make up your own melodies and solos.

IN PRACTICE

Don't try to take in too much of this information at once. Get used to them as finger exercises to start with and then think about the theory behind it all.

STEP 1

Pick a key. Let's say B. Find that note on the seventh fret of the E string.

STEP 2

Now select a scale. I choose the major scale. The black dot has a '2' in it so fret the string with your second finger.

STEP 3

Now play each successive note up the scale. That will be fourth finger on the ninth fret of the E string, first finger on sixth fret of the A string, second finger on the seventh fret of the A string, and so on. We're sticking with the finger-per-fret technique here so your hand shouldn't be jumping around the neck too much.

STEP 4

When you get to the last note on the high E string, work your way back down to the beginning.

STEP 5

Pick another key and scale to go again! Always play the scales from the black dot otherwise you won't be hearing it in the right context.

CD TRACK 27

TIP

Strum the chord first to tune your ear to the key you are playing in. Try to find notes and shapes that you like over certain chords. The ones that you memorise and use will help to form your own unique style. When you are used to the shapes, try playing the notes in different orders for more interesting sounds. Make your own tunes and solos.

EXERCISE

It's good to start off practising scales by going up and down the shapes. These exercises are all in the key of A. Try to hear the flavours that each scale gives.

1. An A minor chord followed by the A minor pentatonic.

2. An A major chord followed by the A major pentatonic.

TRACK 28 CD

Do you spot any similarities between the two pentatonic scales? You should see that the shapes are the same but the root notes start in different places. Easy to remember, huh?

3. An A major chord followed by the A major scale.

TRACK 29 CD

PROBLEM?

Finding things a bit dull? Keep in mind that running through scales teaches you a lot. You are continuing to build strength and developing your fretting and picking technique. Hearing the sounds of these scales trains your ears, which will help you to improvise and write melodies. This stuff gets you another step closer to that marathon guitar solo under the stage spotlight!

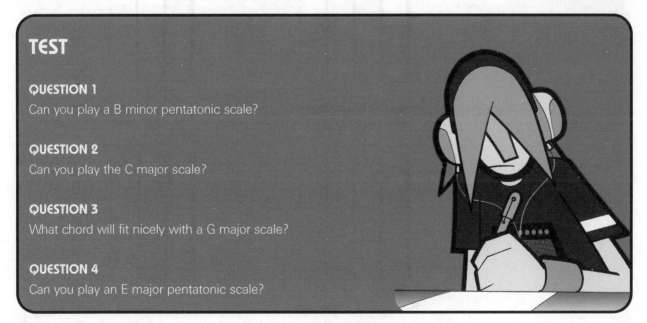

TEST

QUESTION 1
Can you play a B minor pentatonic scale?

QUESTION 2
Can you play the C major scale?

QUESTION 3
What chord will fit nicely with a G major scale?

QUESTION 4
Can you play an E major pentatonic scale?

MOVEABLE CHORDS

This lesson is going to introduce you to the chord of rock – the 5-chord! We'll also expand the shape into a full 'barre' chord and discover how using just a few shapes can give us many chords. Plug in all your effects pedals and crank up the distortion my fellow stringsters!

YOUR GOALS

GOAL 1
To learn some moveable chord shapes.

GOAL 2
To increase hand strength.

GOAL 3
To practise that fretboard knowledge.

GOAL 4
To rrrrrrock on!

THEORY

You've now seen that we can move one scale shape anywhere on the neck to play in the desired key. These moveable chords use the same principle. Have a look at the chord diagrams and focus on the black dot for your root note. If you start with the black dot on the fifth fret of the E string, you're playing an A chord. With the black dot on the eighth fret, you're playing a C.

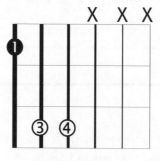

5-chord (E string root)

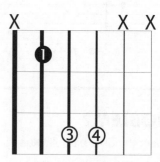

5-chord (A string root)

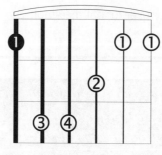

E-shape Major barre

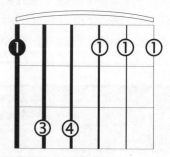

E-shape Minor barre

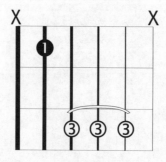

A-shape Major barre

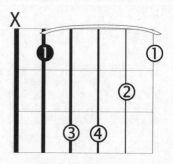

A-shape Minor barre

We also have some shapes where the black dot is on the A string. So starting on the fifth fret of the A string (have you learned you're A string notes yet?!) we get a D chord. Remember not to strum any strings with an 'X' above.

Looking at the 5-chord you'll see there are only three strings involved. With only a few notes being played it means you can stick your amp overdrive at ten and get some really cool sounds. Loads of rock tunes use this shape and it's not too hard on the fingers.

Now, the guitar has six strings but we've only got four fingers – yikes! We handle this by having one finger 'barre' across a number of strings. You're using the length of your finger rather than the fingertip to do this – check the photos. When your finger has to barre the strings you'll see a line going across the fret on the diagram.

5-chord

E-shape Major barre

A-shape Major barre

Do you see any similarities with the shapes in the barre chords and the open chords? The barres with the root on the E string come from the open E chord shapes. The barres with the root on the A string come from the open A chord shapes.

PROBLEM?

Barre chords are much trickier than open chords because you have to fret more strings. Get used to the principles of moveable chords with the easier 5-chord and then concentrate on getting those big barre chords mastered. If it doesn't sound right, pick each string individually to check it's ringing. Go back to the old open chord problem checklist.

TIP

Suppose that your song goes from G5 to C5. You can play the G from the third fret of the E string and then the C from the third fret of the A string – your hand has hardly moved!

TEST

QUESTION 1
Within the first 12 frets, how many D minor chords can you play now?

QUESTION 2
Where is the root note in the A minor shape barre chord?

QUESTION 3
How can you mute the strings with your fret hand?

QUESTION 4
Within the first 12 frets, how many F major chords can you play?

IN PRACTICE

Hopefully your hands are getting stronger now so it's time to put them to the test. Pushing all the strings down can be hard work but, as always, it does get easier with practice. Go careful and remember to keep the thumb behind the neck for good support and less pain.

STEP 1

5-chords first. Get your fret hand in the glove-puppet-biting-the-neck position! Pick a key. Let's say B. We find that note on the seventh fret of the E string so the first finger goes there and the third and fourth fingers fall into the 5-chord shape below it. Give it a strum.

STEP 2

Now let's find the note B on the A string. Second fret, yeah? Get your first finger in position and again the third and fourth fingers follow its lead. Give this one a strum and it should sound the same. It's the same chord but in a different position on the neck.

STEP 3

Now lets try an A major with the E-barre shape. Get your first finger on the fifth fret of the E string, but barring across all six strings – ow! Give them a strum and see how it's doing. It'll be tricky for a bit until your finger toughens up.

STEP 4

With your first finger doing the barre work, get the other three into the rest of the E shape. Note that with these fingers in position, your first finger can just concentrate on the low E, B and high E strings.

STEP 5

So that was an A major. We learned A major as an open chord, didn't we? Compare the two and see how similar they sound. See if you can find the barre chord equivalents to all the open chords we learned earlier.

EXERCISE

1. Try this exercise that moves up the neck with the 5-chord shape. As you prepare to move to the next chord, lock your fingers rigidly into the shape and slide the whole hand up to the next fret.

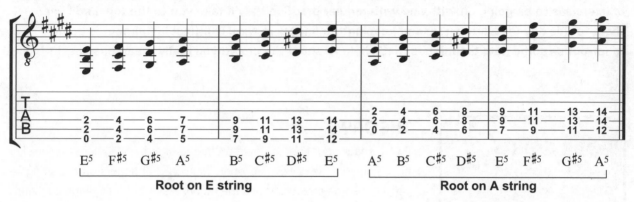

TRACK 30

2. Here's a chord progression using the 5-chords. Pay attention to the rhythms.

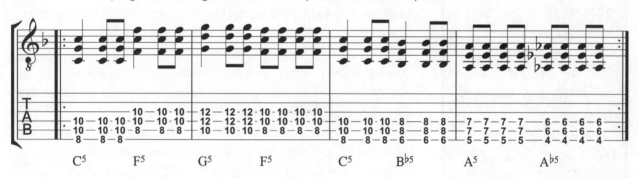

TRACK 31

3. Try playing each of the barre chords below.

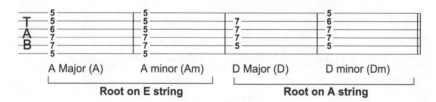

TRACK 32

4. This exercise is similar to the 5-chord progression but expanded to include full barre chords. There are a lot of notes notated here but you'll get used to relating the number patterns back to the chord diagrams.

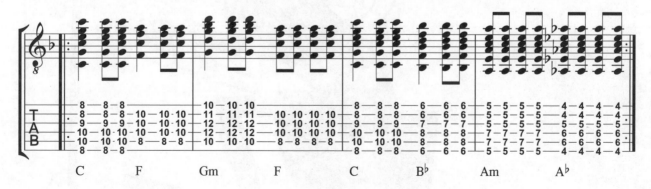

TRACK 33

TECHNIQUES

Whoa, our last lesson! It's been good fun showing you the ropes (or strings). You've got loads of exercises to be going on with and with regular practice they'll take you to the top. I still use them to this day for warming up and keeping the fingers in trim. Our final instalment is going to introduce some new techniques that'll help to show the crowd you really mean business!

YOUR GOALS

GOAL 1
To nail the 'hammer-on'.

GOAL 2
To perfect the 'pull-off'.

GOAL 3
To combine the two.

GOAL 4
And finally…to experiment! Make as much new stuff up as you can! Go forth and widdle!

THEORY

If you whack your fingers down on the fretboard, you'll more than likely hear a note or two. Likewise, when you pull your fingers off the strings you'll get some sounds. That's the theory really, but let's refine it a little!

The 'hammer-on' is the technique of fretting the string quickly and firmly to make a note. The fretted note should sound without the need for a separate pick stroke.

Opposite to the hammer-on is the 'pull-off'. When your finger is already fretting a string, pull it off at an angle so you lightly pluck it and sound the lower note. Again, no need for an extra pick.

Repeating the two techniques one after the other will create a series of notes without the need to pick at all. If you can master this, your picking hand will be free to flick the hair out of your eyes! Hmmmm – I should be keeping tips like these to myself!

These methods are shown on TAB by a tie line linking two or more notes together. So, you pick the first note and then hammer-on or pull-off to the note tied to it. You'll usually see an 'H' or 'PO' written above the tie too.

IN PRACTICE

Work through these steps and before you know it you'll be booking a place in the World's Strongest Finger Championships!

STEP 1

Put your first finger on the fifth fret of any string and pick it. Whilst the note is still ringing, hammer your second finger down quite hard onto the sixth fret. You should hear the note go up.

STEP 2

If you keep going between these two notes the pattern is 'pick, hammer, pick, hammer' and so on. Do this at regular time intervals like we've been doing with previous exercises. If you start to trip up, slow right down and make sure each note is played evenly and clearly.

STEP 3

This time put your first finger on the fifth fret and second finger on the sixth at the same time. Pick the note and pull your second finger away at about 45 degrees from the fretboard so that string is plucked and the fifth fret note rings out.

STEP 4

Repeat the pattern as we did with the hammer-on steps – 'pick, pull-off, pick, pull-off'.

STEP 5

With a grasp of those two actions, try to link the hammer-on and the pull-off together. You'll probably need to pick to start them off but can then go with the pattern 'hammer, pull-off, hammer, pull-off'.

EXERCISE

1. Here are four separate hammer-on exercises between the repeat marks – keep going round and round each one for a good 20 seconds to build up finger strength and speed. Pay attention to the fingers to use (numbered above the TAB) and also when to pick (indicated below the TAB).

2. These contain a group of four pull-off exercises with similar patterns to the last. The same rules apply!

3. The two techniques are combined in these exercises. Remember, start yourself off with a single pick and then let the hammer-ons and pull-offs do the work. See how many repetitions you can do before the sound fades.

4. These exercises introduce an extra finger to the mix.

When you've got the idea of each exercise, try the patterns on different frets and strings. Remember that frets higher up the neck are less of a stretch.

TEST

QUESTION 1
Does a hammer-on make the previous note go up or down?

QUESTION 2
Should you practise hammer-ons and pull-offs with all fingers?

QUESTION 3
Does a pull-off make the previous note go up or down?

Look back through the previous lessons. When you've got more than one note on a string, try to incorporate the hammer-ons and pull-offs instead of picking everything. See how it sounds and affects your playing.

TOP 10 ARTISTS

TOM DELONGE

Tom Delonge is guitar and vocals for the energetic punk trio Blink 182. Tom was 14 when he met up with bass player Mark Hoppus and drummer Scott Raynor in San Diego, California. Their first gig was at a tiny bar in 1992 where nobody showed up, but the bartender gave some words of encouragement and they carried on. They began putting out recordings in 1993 with an EP and cassette demo, which then led to their first full track release in 1994. Tom's high-speed riffing got the tracks onto a number of extreme sports videos and started a following. Popularity grew with the commercial success of *Dude Ranch* in 1997, and they were hearing their melodic, thrashy tunes more and more over the radio airwaves. Blink have six albums under their belt but Tom has also found the time to run a side-project band called Box Car Racer where he puts some of his heavier tunes to good use.

LISTEN TO

'All The Small Things'
'What's My Name Again'
'First Date'
'Feeling This'

STATISTICS

DATE OF BIRTH
13 December 1975

PLACE OF BIRTH
San Diego, California

GENRE
Punk pop

INFLUENCES
Beastie Boys, Descendents, NOFX, Nirvana

FIRST HIT
'Dammit (Growing Up)'

HIGHEST CHART POSITION
'All The Small Things' –
UK #2 – 2000

IN THE STYLE OF...

Tom and Blink 182 have given us some fast-paced, tuneful rock tracks. He comes up with song ideas acoustically and puts them to the volume test when the parts are ready. His early guitar sounds were from a Fender Stratocaster with one humbucker pickup fitted, but recently he's gone for a custom semi-hollow Gibson. Dial up plenty of distortion on your amp and try turning the Mid control down.

HOW TO PLAY LIKE TOM DELONGE

This is a typical Blink chugging rhythm guitar example, making maximum use of the 5-chord. The 'MU' indicates that this is all muted, which you can do by resting the palm of your picking hand lightly on the strings. For the punky sound, try to pick all the notes with downstrokes. Don't worry too much about any noise between changing chords as this all adds to the energy.

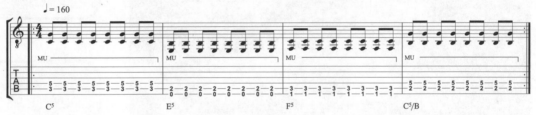

Here's a little melody that will fit nicely over the chord sequence above. It's basically following the top two strings of the complete chords.

When you get used to this line, try doubling up the speed to match the eighth notes of the rhythm guitar.

TRACKS 38 & 39

TRUE STORY!

Blink 182 were originally just called Blink, but they soon learned of another band with the same name. Sticking the number on the end didn't lose them too many fans.

SUPERSTAR TIP!

To get the energy of Tom's speedy tracks across, the rhythm needs to be tight. Ensure that fast riffs are in time with everything else in the band otherwise it will just sound a mess.

NOEL GALLAGHER

Noel Gallagher is the guitarist and songwriter from Oasis, who are often compared to the one and only Beatles. He taught himself guitar at the age of 13 by working out his favourite songs. After failing an audition for Manchester-based band Inspiral Carpets, he got the next best thing – to be their roadie. Nowadays he has people to carry around his own stuff. Noel joined up with his brother Liam on vocals to bring rock 'n' roll to the '90s. They named the band Oasis, after a leisure centre. In a relatively short time the Gallagher brothers have enjoyed a string of hit singles and five successful albums. If it's catchy sing-alongs you're after, look no further.

LISTEN TO

'Wonderwall'
'Stand By Me'
'Roll With It'
'Little By Little'

STATISTICS

DATE OF BIRTH
29 May 1967

PLACE OF BIRTH
Manchester, England

GENRE
Brit rock

INFLUENCES
The Beatles, The Stone Roses, The Rolling Stones

FIRST HIT
'Live Forever'

HIGHEST CHART POSITION
#1 on many occasions

IN THE STYLE OF...

With Mr Gallagher we're talking catchy chord sequences and melodies. The sort of things to which you might say, 'Why didn't I think of that?' Noel has been known to use a range of guitars including the Les Paul, particularly on the early album *Definitely Maybe*. Are you mad for it?

HOW TO PLAY LIKE NOEL GALLAGHER

One technique is to use chords that keep some of the fingers in the same place throughout. This gives the effect of a nice regular tone whilst the bass notes move around for a melody. So, this example keeps the third and fourth fingers in the same area of the B and high E strings. The strumming pattern is important too, emphasising the bass notes at the start of each bar.

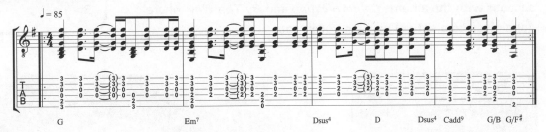

Noel's best friend is the major pentatonic scale shape as seen in the scale lesson. This solo section makes use of just that – the G major pentatonic. You could pick all the notes, but ideally use hammer-ons and pull-offs where indicated to help it flow smoothly. There's an 'S' in the last bar too indicating a 'slide'. Get your finger down on the 14th fret and, whilst keeping it down, slide your hand up until it reaches the 16th – a rigid finger is required.

TRACKS 40 & 41

JOHN FRUSCIANTE

John Frusciante is the funky punky guitar man from the Red Hot Chili Peppers. He was not an original member of the band though – they have gone through their fair share of guitarists in the past. John developed his distinctive style from a diet of punk, funk and some very technical musicians such as Frank Zappa and Steve Vai. The opportunity to jam with Flea on bass and Chad on drums can also have done him no end of good. He first joined the Chili's at the age of 18 for their album *Mothers Milk* which featured a cover of the Stevie Wonder track 'Higher Ground'. Their next album in 1991 was to be the biggy though – *Blood Sugar Sex Magik*. However, John left the band mid-tour in 1992, giving us a couple of solo albums in the break. After the Peppers released another album with Jane's Addiction guitarist, Dave Navarro, John made his return to the Peppers. They since enjoyed further success with the albums *Californication* and *By The Way* where John gives us plenty of backing vocals too.

LISTEN TO

'Higher Ground'
'Under The Bridge'
'Scar Tissue'
'By The Way'

STATISTICS

DATE OF BIRTH
5 March 1970

PLACE OF BIRTH
New York, USA

GENRE
Funk rock

INFLUENCES
Jimi Hendrix, Jimmy Page,
Frank Zappa, Steve Vai,
Black Flag

FIRST HIT
'Give It Away'

HIGHEST CHART POSITION
'Under The Bridge' –
US #2 – 1992

IN THE STYLE OF...

John's riffs are hard-hitting but often quite simple, carefully placed amongst Flea's bass lines. Let's get the funk out.

HOW TO PLAY LIKE JOHN FRUSCIANTE

Here's an example of a cool funk rhythm played with a diad (two notes). It doubles up on the eighth notes that we learned in the strumming lesson to make 'sixteenth' notes. There are now four hits per beat which can be counted as '1 ee and a, 2 ee and a, 3 ee and a, 4 ee and a'. Strum it with the alternate 'down, up, down, up' pattern and you'll find that the picking pattern on the TAB falls into place. The 'CO' sign means 'cut off'. Those notes shouldn't be allowed to ring out for long. Cut them short by releasing the pressure in your fretting hand.

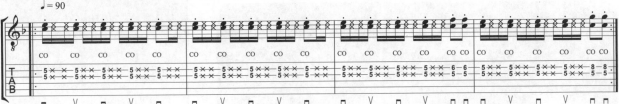

This next part is a more melodic exercise. There's a big interval between the two notes and hence a big string skip. Be careful that your pick doesn't hit the strings in-between. Alternatively, pick the A string with the pick as normal and pluck the B string with the second finger of your picking hand.

TRACKS 42 & 43

TRUE STORY!

For the multi-million selling album *Blood Sugar Sex Magik*, the Chili's producer Rick Rubin had the band and recording equipment move into a haunted mansion. Live the music!

SUPERSTAR TIP!

John's funky, twangy sound comes from hitting the strings of his Fender with a lot of snap. Imagine trying to shake a bit of sticky tape off your fingers – that's the sort of motion we're after!

SLASH

The sight of a Les Paul guitar supported by big hair and a top hat can only mean one thing! Slash got his first guitar when in junior high. Self-taught by listening to records and working out the parts for himself, he formed his first band. It was through this that he met the other members of Guns N' Roses. After four successful albums with Guns N' Roses in the late '80s and early '90s he moved off to form Slash's Snakepit and released another couple of albums in 1995 and 2000. More recently, Slash has reunited with former Guns N' Roses colleagues Duff McKagan (bass) and Matt Sorum (drums) for the band Velvet Revolver. Slash is renowned for his catchy soloing with a bluesy edge and of course his distinctive look. He has also made various guest appearances on tracks such as Michael Jackson's 'Black or White'.

LISTEN TO

'Sweet Child O' Mine'
'Paradise City'
'You Could Be Mine'

STATISTICS

DATE OF BIRTH
23 July 1965

PLACE OF BIRTH
Stoke-on-Trent, England

GENRE
Hard rock

INFLUENCES
Led Zeppelin, Jimi Hendrix, Jeff Beck, The Rolling Stones

FIRST HIT
'Sweet Child O' Mine'

HIGHEST CHART POSITION
'Sweet Child O' Mine
– US #1 – 1988

TRUE STORY!

Believe it or not, Slash is a nickname that was given to him by a friend! He was actually born with the name Saul Hudson.

SUPERSTAR TIP!

How does Slash see through all that hair? Well, maybe he doesn't!? He says that he doesn't know any of the theory behind what he plays, so it must be by ear. Train your ear by singing along with the notes that you play and working out other people's music for yourself.

IN THE STYLE OF...

HOW TO PLAY LIKE SLASH

Guns N' Roses liked their mix of clean and heavy guitar parts. This first line is a picking pattern around some open chords. The last bar sneaks in a couple of hammer-ons and pull-offs near where the fingers are in the chord shape.

To rock it up, here are some big power chords that follow along with the clean stuff. The shapes are the same as the open chords we've met but pay attention to the strings that aren't numbered – stop these ones from ringing by resting a spare bit of finger lightly to mute. The 'X' symbols indicate percussive chugs (mute again) which say to the listener, 'Here comes another big chord'!

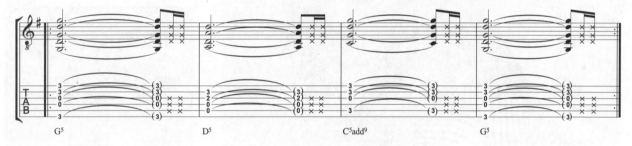

Mr Slash is another one for the major pentatonic scale, and he puts it to good use in a bluesy rock kind of style. This example introduces the 'BU' and 'LD' signs – 'Bend Upwards' and 'Let Down'. Fret the first note and then push the string across the fretboard (towards the ceiling) so the string is bent and the note goes up. Your finger needs to dig in so as not to lose grip. The target note is the one in brackets (try fretting it to hear where you're heading).

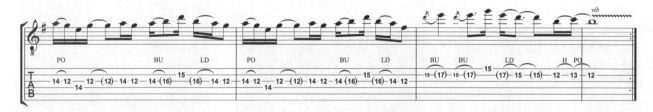

KURT COBAIN

Kurt brought grunge music to MTV and showed us that you don't need to widdle to be a guitar hero. He bought his first six-string when he was 14 and learned a few chords. After doing a bit of roadie work, he set up the band Nirvana in 1986. They became well known for their tuneful melodies backed by heavy guitar. After the first album, *Bleach*, in 1989 they were onto their sixth drummer, Dave Grohl, now of The Foo Fighters. With this final band line-up they became world famous with the second album, *Nevermind*, in 1991. One week before Kurt died in 1994 they played an MTV unplugged gig, and it was later released as a final memory.

LISTEN TO

'Smells Like Teen Spirit'
'In Bloom'
'About A Girl'
'Heart-Shaped Box'

SUPERSTAR TIP!

Kurt always avoided the guitar hero label saying that he could barely play the thing himself. He did acknowledge that the more technical guitarists out there wouldn't be able to play the guitar like he does though.

STATISTICS

DATE OF BIRTH
20 February 1967

PLACE OF BIRTH
Aberdeen, Washington, USA

GENRE
Grunge

INFLUENCES
Mark Lanegan, Frank Black, Iggy Pop, Tony Iommi

FIRST HIT
'Smells Like Teen Spirit'

HIGHEST CHART POSITION
'Heart-Shaped Box' –
UK #5 – 1993

IN THE STYLE OF...

Cobain's style of playing showed us that you don't need an expensive guitar and years of practice to get something big out of the instrument. If you're playing along with the Nirvana tracks, be aware that some of them were recorded with different tunings – sometimes all the strings were tuned down a semitone or two.

HOW TO PLAY LIKE KURT COBAIN

The first example is all about attitude. Think of something that annoys you and take it out on the strings! Grip the pick with more of a fist and use your whole arm for the strums. The occasional open string or noisy chord change is fine because that just helps to show how angry you are! It's the trusty 5-chords for Kurt and plenty of percussive, muted strums where you see the 'X' symbols. There's a cheeky bend thrown in to finish the sequence off.

A few Nirvana tracks use a tuning called 'drop D' and so the next exercise demonstrates just that. Instead of tuning the low E string to E you drop it a tone (two frets) to D. Check it's correct by comparing to the other D string – they should sound an octave apart. The lower note adds to the aggression and also makes a 5-chord slightly easier to play – all the notes are now on the same fret.

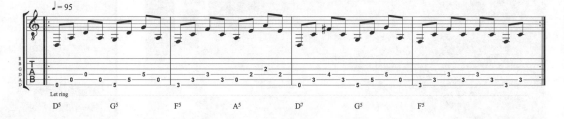

TRUE STORY!
Making successful songs can be done on the cheap. Nirvana's first album, *Bleach*, cost a mere $600 to record and it is said that the song 'Polly' from the album, *Nevermind*, was played on a $20 guitar!

THE EDGE

Dave Evans is the man behind the stage name The Edge. He started out in music with guitar and piano lessons. At the age of 16 he spotted an advert at school looking to set up a band and so met up with the others for a jam. They set out by playing covers of Rolling Stones', Beatles' and Beach Boys' tunes and finally settled on the name U2. Their big break came when they won a talent contest in 1978. This hooked them up with a manager that got them signed in Ireland to CBS Records. The first EP came out in 1979, and they have been releasing chart-busting albums regularly ever since. Hearing one blast of The Edge's unique guitar style will tell you exactly who it is. His keyboard skills also get an outing every now and then.

LISTEN TO

'Pride'
'Desire'
'I Still Haven't Found What I'm Looking For'
'Beautiful Day'

STATISTICS

DATE OF BIRTH
8 August 1961

PLACE OF BIRTH
Essex, England

GENRE
Alternative rock/pop

INFLUENCES
The Who, The Sex Pistols, David Bowie, Thin Lizzy

FIRST HIT
'New Year's Day'

HIGHEST CHART POSITION
#1 on many occasions

IN THE STYLE OF...

Sometimes you may not realise U2's sounds are coming from a guitar. The Edge certainly has an instantly recognisable style. One part of his signature sound is from the clever use of delay-effect pedals. If you're feeling lazy, plug one in and you get two or more notes for the price of one!

HOW TO PLAY LIKE THE EDGE

When you've got such a great tone and a nice supply of FX pedals, too many notes can sometimes spoil the end result. Here's a three-string exercise taking us around a progression of four chords – G, D, A and B minor. If you've got a delay effect in your pedal collection, experiment!

The next example uses the same chord structure but whizzes higher up the neck. This leaves the bass player to do the low notes whilst you deal with the chiming high-end chords. Watch the picking pattern here – keep your arm ticking up and down and you'll find the notes fall into place.

TRACKS 50 & 51

CD

SUPERSTAR TIP!

The Edge pays great attention to his sounds, looking for unusual effects that inspire and blow your mind. Getting a good sound can help you to create new ideas and tunes.

TOM MORELLO

Tom's the chap with a cap and guitar high on it's strap. Sometimes he plays the guitar like the rest of us but a lot of the time he goes for more adventurous sounds like a ringing bell, wailing police siren or squealing cat. Cooool! He got into rock music in his teens, teaching himself guitar and sometimes practising eight hours a day. After university, Morello moved to Los Angeles to pursue music. When his first band broke up, Tom met up with new members to form Rage Against The Machine. With a rap vocalist, bass, drums and Tom's unique guitar style it was a new sound for the '90s. Rage Against The Machine released four successful albums before the vocalist Zack de la Rocha left them. He was promptly replaced with Chris Cornell, former singer of Soundgarden. The band were then renamed Audioslave. May the crazy sounds continue.

LISTEN TO

'Killing In The Name'
'Bombtrack'
'Bulls On Parade'
'Cochise'

STATISTICS

DATE OF BIRTH
30 May 1964

PLACE OF BIRTH
New York, USA

GENRE
Alternative metal

INFLUENCES
Wes Montgomery, Jimmy Page, Al Di Meola, Dave Gilmour

FIRST HIT
'Killing In The Name'

HIGHEST CHART POSITION
'Bulls On Parade' –
UK #8 – 1996

IN THE STYLE OF...

Tom's rhythm guitar parts are raw rock riffs that follow the bass guitar closely, giving the songs a fat sound. For solos we are treated to r-r-record-scratching-style stuff. Don't be scared off, it's not just the fingers that he's using. His tricks include scraping the strings, playing around with an effect pedal called 'whammy' and flicking the pickups on and off. Is there anything left for us to invent?

HOW TO PLAY LIKE TOM MORELLO

Here we have a typical Tom-style riff. The notes involved here are mainly from the E minor pentatonic. A nice idea, which appears in bar two, is to double up the single notes with the octave – we look at this shape in the fretboard lesson. You can strum across all three strings in the octave shape if you mute the string in-between with the bottom of your first fretting finger. This example finishes off with a 'natural harmonic' at the fifth fret. Do this by lightly resting a finger directly over the fifth-fret wire – you should get a really high note.

Just like Kurt Cobain, Tom has been known to use the 'drop D' tuning (check the Kurt style). So, lower the E string and try using a first-finger barre to fret the following riff.

KIRK HAMMETT

Kirk Hammett was given a promising start by having guitar lessons from the maestro, Joe Satriani. His next bit of luck was in 1983 when members of Metallica spotted him playing for a rock band called Exodus. They were replacing their previous guitarist Dave Mustaine, who went on to form Megadeth. After a quick audition, it was clear that Kirk was just what Metallica were looking for. He took a while to apply his mixture of thrash and blues because the first album *Kil 'em All* was already written. The next albums *Ride The Lightning* and *Master Of Puppets* were where he made his mark, building a fine guitar partnership with James Hetfield. The band nearly split up whilst touring in 1986 when their tour bus crashed, killing bass player Cliff Burton. However, the decision was made to carry on and new bassist Jason Newstead took the place. Metallica went from strength to strength, fully establishing themselves with 1988's *And Justice For All* and a further five albums throughout the '90s.

LISTEN TO

'Sad But True'
'Enter Sandman'
'Until It Sleeps'
'St Anger'

STATISTICS

DATE OF BIRTH
18 November 1962

PLACE OF BIRTH
San Francisco, USA

GENRE
Metal

INFLUENCES
Eddie Van Halen, Jimi Hendrix, Scott Gorham, Joe Satriani

FIRST HIT
'Enter Sandman'

HIGHEST CHART POSITION
'Enter Sandman' – UK #5 – 1991

IN THE STYLE OF...

Kirk Hammett has given us a wealth of classic metal riffs. The powerful sound comes from an ESP guitar into an amp with the Gain, Bass and Treble turned up, but Mid turned down. This is how to make your guitar sound angry – raaaaaaah! His style is a blend of thrash and blues, the blues coming out on more recent albums. Listen out for the 'nasty' notes that he fits into the riffs – if you play in the key of E, try the notes without any sharps or flats, as looked at in the fretboard lesson.

HOW TO PLAY LIKE KIRK HAMMETT

First up is a monster riff that would probably be doubled up on guitar by Kirk's bandmate James Hetfield. With the correct sound dialled up on the amp, use your picking hand to mute where indicated. You can get the thrashy attack by almost bouncing your hand onto the strings for the 'X' and mute parts.

Next is a Kirk-style solo idea that will fit over the previous riff in the key of E. The last two bars use a typical lick that fits into the E minor pentatonic shape we learned in the scales lesson. With that in mind, you can take the lick as your own and play it in different keys.

ERIC CLAPTON

Eric Clapton makes the guitar sing! The grandparents out there should listen up – Eric's granny gave him his first guitar when he was 14. He then set about becoming a guitar legend... and succeeded! After regularly playing in pubs and clubs, Clapton crept into fame by joining The Yardbirds. It was here that he gained the nickname 'Slowhand'. The path then took him to *Bluesbreakers*, *Cream* and *Blind Faith* before heading off as a solo act. But, it's not just electric guitar that Eric's famous for. One of his more recent successes was the *Unplugged* acoustic album recorded at an MTV concert in 1992. Eric Clapton's a generous bloke too – in 1999 he auctioned off 100 of his vintage guitars raising more than $5 million for charity.

LISTEN TO

'Layla'
'I Shot The Sheriff'
'Hideaway'
'Crossroads'

STATISTICS

DATE OF BIRTH
30 March 1945

PLACE OF BIRTH
Ripley, Surrey, England

GENRE
Rock, blues

INFLUENCES
Big Bill Broonzy, Muddy Waters, Robert Johnson

FIRST HIT
'For Your Love'

HIGHEST CHART POSITION
'I Shot The Sheriff' – US #1 – 1974

IN THE STYLE OF...

Since the '60s, Eric Clapton has been treating us to some great blues and rock moments. He mixes his notes with controlled vibrato and accurate, tasteful bends. In the early days, Eric would usually be seen with a Gibson Les Paul. These days you'll usually see him with a Fender Stratocaster unless he's on one of his unplugged sets.

HOW TO PLAY LIKE ERIC CLAPTON

If you wanna play the blues you'll need to know the 12-bar chord progression. Here it is in the key of A with some Clapton-style riffing and a solo outro to turn it around.

The feel of the 5-chord riff in the first bar is all about the staccato notes marked with a 'CO'. Cut them short by either releasing the fret hand or bringing the pick hand down onto the strings. You should get a sort of 'Dut Daaaaah Dut Daaaaah' thing going onto the count of '1 and 2 and'. Don't forget to suck in your bottom lip for the tasteful solo bit at the end! It's based around the A minor pentatonic shape learned in the scales lesson.

JIMI HENDRIX

A fair few people will have picked up a guitar because of this guy. Jimi was completely original right down to playing a right-handed guitar left-handed. As a schoolboy, Hendrix taught himself to play the strings and joined up with a few R&B bands. After a brief departure as a parachutist for the air force, he returned to music and began working as a session guitarist – wise choice! This gave a few years of gigging experience with the likes of Tina Turner and eventually led to the meeting of his soon-to-be manager, Chas Chandler, in 1966. They set up The Jimi Hendrix Experience and the rest was to go down in history. Sadly, it was only the next four years of genius that he could give us before he died on 18 September 1970.

LISTEN TO

'Hey Joe'
'Purple Haze'
'Crosstown Traffic'
'Voodoo Chile'

STATISTICS

DATE OF BIRTH
27 November 1942

PLACE OF BIRTH
Seattle, Washington, USA

GENRE
'60s rock

INFLUENCES
Robert Johnson, BB King

FIRST HIT
'Hey Joe'

HIGHEST CHART POSITION
'Voodoo Chile' –
UK #1 – 1970

IN THE STYLE OF...

TRUE STORY!

Jimi became famous not only for his incredible playing and songwriting but also for his lively stage performances. These included playing the guitar behind his back, plucking strings with his teeth and setting the guitar on fire (very cruel, don't try this at home folks).

Prepare to experience... The Jimi Hendrix Experience. Jimi chose a Fender Stratocaster and strained the volume of a nice tube amp to the max so you could hear its pain. Wild vibrato, screaming string bends and a wah-wah pedal – trust me, if you listen to some of his tracks like 'Voodoo Chile', you'll all want one. Wah on dudes.

HOW TO PLAY LIKE JIMI HENDRIX

This is a type of Jimi solo/riff. Get the wah-wah pedal out if you've got one for extra feel and you might be fooled into thinking the guitar is talking. It's based around the E minor pentatonic scale and the last note has a bit of 'vib' added. This is 'vibrato' and is one of the reasons Hendrix is so recognisable. When you pick the note, try shaking the string so that the note wavers up and down slightly. Most of the motion can come from twisting the wrist.

TRACK 60

Next is a clean-sounding progression that makes use of the open chords we look at in the lessons. The strumming pattern hits the bass notes first and then the higher-pitched strings of each chord.

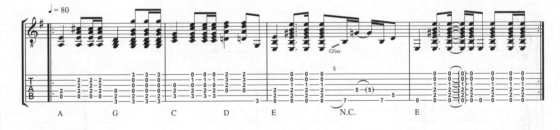

TRACKS 61 & 62

SUPERSTAR TIP!

Hendrix got some cool sounds by flicking the pickup toggle switch up and down quickly and making the guitar feedback by holding the guitar close to its speaker – careful with this.

NOTES

NOTES

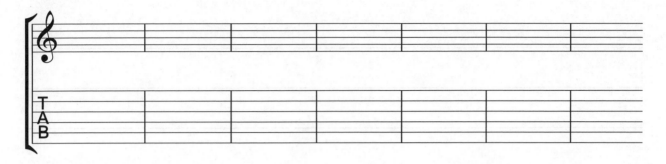

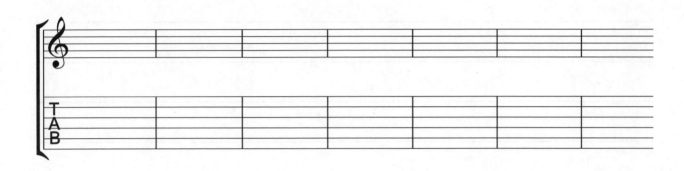

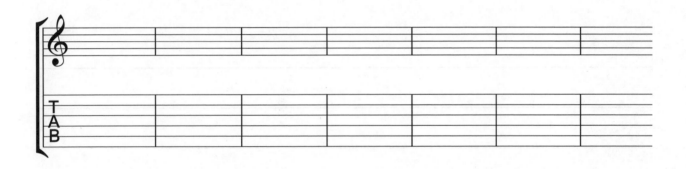

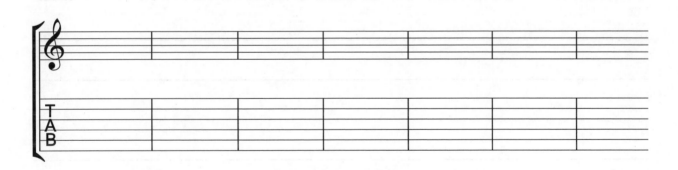

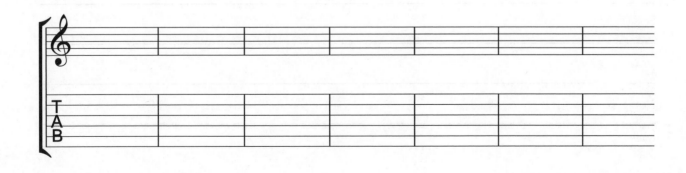

NOTES

GLOSSARY

8VA
The notes indicated on a traditional music stave are played an octave higher than indicated.

5-CHORD
A chord containing just the first and fifth notes of the scale.

ALTERNATE PICKING
To pick repeatedly with a downstroke followed by an upstroke, rather than all in the same direction.

ARPEGGIO
The notes of a chord played individually one after another instead of all at once.

BARRE CHORD
A moveable chord shape where the first finger barres across a number of strings.

BD
'Bend Down' – to bend the string down, in the direction of the floor

BEND
Fret a note and then bend the string so that the pitch is raised.

BU
'Bend Up' – to bend the string up, in the direction of the ceiling.

CAPO
A device for effectively creating a new nut, higher up the neck.

CHORD
A combination of three or more notes played at the same time.

CHROMATIC
A scale that includes all 11 notes.

CO
'Cut Off' – to play a note and quickly cut it short by muting. Also known as Staccato.

CROTCHET
The notation symbol to indicate a quarter note.

DIATONIC
A scale that includes 7 different notes from the available 11.

DROP D
A variation on standard tuning where the low E string is tuned down to D.

FLAT
A note that is lower in pitch.

HAMMER-ON (H)
Making the string sound by hitting it onto the fretboard.

INTERVAL
The distance between one note and another.

LD
'Let Down' – to release an already bent string.

METRONOME
A device that indicates a regular time interval with a click sound or flashing light.

MUTE (MU)
To reduce the vibration of the strings by resting the hand, or the fingers, over them.

NATURAL HARMONIC (NH)
Pick a string whilst lightly touching directly over the suggested fret (5th, 7th or 12th is good).

NC
'No Chord' – to indicate that a chord shouldn't be played over a section of the music.

OPEN
Strings that are played without being fretted.

PENTATONIC
A scale that includes 5 different notes from the available 11.

PULL-OFF (PO)
Making the string sound by quickly pulling the finger away from the fretboard with a light pluck.

QUAVER
The notation symbol to indicate an eighth note.

REST
A notation symbol to indicate a period of silence.

ROOT
The note that a chord or scale is built from.

SEMIQUAVER
The notation symbol to indicate a 16th note.

SEMITONE
The smallest interval available on the guitar – between two neighbouring frets.

SHARP
A note that is raised in pitch.

SLIDE (S)
To fret a note and slide the finger up or down the neck, maintaining the sound throughout.

TEMPO
The speed of the beats in the music, measured in BPM (Beats Per Minute).

TONE
An interval of two semitones or to describe the quality of a sound.

VIBRATO (VIB)
To bend and release the string in small amounts repeatedly.

TIE
The line linking two notes together. Only the first note in the tie is picked – eg a hammer-on. Also used to indicate when a note should continue ringing from one bar to the next.

ANSWERS TO TEST QUESTIONS

LESSON 1 – GET COMFORTABLE
1. Stop playing, stretch out and take a rest.
2. Right-handers on the right leg. Left-handers on the left leg.
3. Keep a part of your picking hand in contact with the guitar.
4. Right-handers pick with the right hand. Left-handers use the left hand.

LESSON 2 – TUNE UP
1. Every Angry Dog Growls Before Eating.
2. The B string.
3. The 5th fret.
Ear training CD:
Sharp
In tune
Sharp
Flat
Flat
In tune
In tune
Flat
Sharp
Flat

LESSON 3 – PICKING
1. The pointed end.
2. Anchor your little finger down on the guitar body or rest the heel of your hand on the bridge.
3. A metronome, drum machine or piece of music with an even tempo.
4. Very efficient, improves speed.

LESSON 4 – FRETTING
1. Just before the fret wire.
2. Usually the third or fourth finger.
3. Very efficient. The hand can stay still and you can find any of the frets under the fingers without looking.

LESSON 5 – OPEN CHORDS
1. Happy.
2. Minor.
3. Don't play the note that the 'X' is above.
Ear training CD:
Minor
Major
Minor
Major
Major
Major
Minor
Minor
Major
Minor

LESSON 6 – STRUMMING
1. A quarter note. One count.
2. V
3. Rest either hand lightly over the strings to stop them vibrating.
4. For example '1 and 2 and 3 and 4 and'.

LESSON 7 – KNOW THE FRETBOARD
1. 'B to C' and 'E to F'.
2. B.

LESSON 8 – SCALES
3. G major.

LESSON 9 – MOVEABLE CHORDS
1. Three – the open chord, the E minor barre shape at the tenth fret and the A minor barre shape at the fifth fret.
2. On the A string.
3. Release the pressure on the strings so that they leave the fret wire.
4. Two – the E major barre shape at the second fret and the A major barre shape at the ninth fret.

LESSON 10 – TECHNIQUES
1. Up.
2. Yes, get all those fingers involved!
3. Down.